Fans of My Unconscious

Fans of My Unconscious

Krista Lukas

Rainshadow Editions
The Black Rock Press
University of Nevada, Reno
2013

ISBN: 978-1-891033-62-9

Library of Congress Control Number: 2013935175

Printed in the United States of America

The Black Rock Press
University of Nevada, Reno
Reno, NV 89557-0224
www.blackrockpress.org

Cover photo of author by Doug Deacy

In memory of my grandparents,
Benson J. Benjamin (1911–2002) and
Leone A. Benjamin (1916–2007)

Contents

III.

IV.

Acknowledgments

Grateful acknowledgement to the editors of the magazines and anthologies in which the following poems first appeared, some in earlier forms and/or under different titles:

5 AM: "Blood Orange"
Aethlon: "Lion on Gold Coast" and "Swimming Inside the Lines"
Chaffin Journal: "War, Hunger, and Accidents Aside"
Chiron Review: "True Is What You Remember"
Eclipse: "Morning"
Edge: "Baby Shower" and "Hotel Casino"
International Psychoanalysis: "The Counselor," "Letter V," and "The Reception"
Jewish Women's Literary Annual: "Leone to Ben"
Kokanee: "Only Now," "The Day I Die," and "Would It Be So Wrong"
Ledge: "No Longer Miss B"
Meadow: "The First Year"
Margie: "Everything Must Go," "I Dream of Osama bin Laden," and "Letter from My Ancestors"
New Millennium Writings: "Vade Mecum"
Ouroboros Review: "My Niece"
Pearl: "Smile Lines"
Quay: "September"
Quercus Review: "Contributors' Notes" and "Fire"
Rattle: "Patio Tomatoes"
Red Rock Review: "Meadow's Rules"
Redivider: "Forever Stamp"
Sierra Nevada Review: "After" and "Twelve Days of Christmas"
Two Review: "What's Best"

"Letter from My Ancestors" was reprinted in *The Best American Poetry* 2006 (Scribner, 2006); *Creative Writer's Handbook*, 5th ed. (Pearson, Prentice Hall, 2009); and *New Poets of the American West* (Many Voices Press, 2010).

"Everything Was Oddly the Same," was shown in the traveling exhibit Always Lost: A Meditation on War.

Grants from the Nevada Arts Council and the Sierra Arts Foundation facilitated the preparation of this manuscript. It was a finalist for the 2009 May Swenson Poetry Award and the 2011 Pearl Poetry Prize.

Information in my poem, "Contributors' Notes," including some similar phrasing, comes from the anthology *Poetry 180*, edited by Billy Collins (Random House, 2003).

I wish to thank my friends for their advice on individual poems; Teresa Breeden, Shaun Griffin, and Suzanne Roberts for helping to shape the manuscript; and Joe Crowley and Bob Blesse for bringing this book into being. Thank you also to my family and my husband, Scott Lukas, for encouragement.

I.

Letter from My Ancestors

We wouldn't write this,
wouldn't even think of it. We are working
people without time on our hands. In the Old Country,

we milk cows or deliver the mail or leave,
scattering to South Africa, Connecticut, Missouri,
and finally, California for the Gold Rush—

Aaron and Lena run the Yosemite campground, general
store, a section of the stagecoach line. Morris comes
later, after the earthquake, finds two irons

and a board in the rubble of San Francisco.
Plenty of prostitutes need their dresses pressed, enough
to earn him the cash to open a haberdashery and marry

Sadie—we all have stories, yes, but we're not thinking
stories. We have work to do, and a dozen children. They'll
go on to pound nails and write up deals, not musings.

We document transactions. Our diaries record
temperatures, landmarks, symptoms. We
do not write our dreams. We place another order,

make the next delivery, save the next
dollar, give another generation—you,
maybe—the luxury of time

to write about us.

Forever Stamp

Is that a guarantee?
> —Grandpa Ben's response at age eighty-seven
> when the DMV clerk handed him his renewed
> driver's license and said, "This one's good for
> another four years."

I have the same question
about the Forever Stamp, *USA First-Class*
written alongside the cracked Liberty Bell.
Forty-two cents, good for an ounce.
Good through the depletion
of fossil fuels, the rise of oceans,
the desert's expansion, the disappearance
of the atmosphere as we know it;
good in domes and through world wars.
Accepted by all mail carriers
in all countries for all time, none of whom
will ever laugh in the face of an optimist
who once invested in stickers.
Good through exponential growth,
the spread of new viruses, meteors,
A-bombs and H-bombs, letter bombs,
the nuclear winter, the return to sticks and stones.
Good when only cockroaches remain,
scuttling in the rubble, to find Forever Stamps
so they can mail themselves to planets
with younger stars for suns.

Blood Orange

Citrus sinensis, pomelo and tangerine,
offspring of ancient Arabian lemons
and Crusader-planted Portogallos.
Pitted skin or smooth, modern
hybrids from Italy, Spain, California—
Khanpur, Ruby, Delphino,
Vaccaro, Sanguinea Doble Fina,
Cara Cara, and the three commonest:

> Moro rinds have veins
> the color of red wine, flesh
> of ruby to vermillion to crimson,
> nearly black. Tarocco is Sicilian
> for beautiful. With a Brix-to-acid ratio
> greater than twelve, the sweetest
> and thinnest skinned, easy to peel.
> The Sanguinello has few seeds, tender flesh,
> long life; ripens by February, remains
> unharvested until April, good until June.

Full-bloods, half-bloods, true bloods,
and look-alikes, per the presence
of anthocyanin versus lycopene.
Stained or unstained rinds
may belie the color of the fruit.
But for hints of raspberry,
their flesh compares to the typical
Valencia or Navel, tasted blind.

How so, then, the given name?
Simple ingredient of cocktails,
marmalade, and gelato, called by only
two words to mean so many. Peeled,
sliced, crushed for the juice—
this body of a seed plant,
shape of the earth, an imperfect
sphere, neither blood, nor orange.

Fire

I watch the campfire, the only light
besides the moon, alluring
luminous flicker, and I want it
simply to be fire, to watch
the dance, the glowing
embers, the smolder, the billowing
smoke, without regret
that there's nothing
new I can say about fire. I want

not to feel the need
to say something,
but for it simply to be
fire without my pausing to recall
it's an element, as in
earth, water, air, and.

I want not to think
of my distant ancestors,
subject of myths, who stole
and later learned to make fire,
and control it, and how without fire,
they never would have developed
civilization to a point where
I consider it a vacation to cook
over open flames and sleep on the ground.

How is it that fire goes from nothing
into something? It's not there,
and then it is, ethereal
never in one place long enough
to make you look away.

Contributors' Notes

What I love is reading
that besides getting fellowships and awards,
the poet has worked
in a steel mill, like Timothy Russell;
or that Ronald Koertge is a devoted handicapper
known to drive miles in bad weather
to get a bet down, or best of all,
something to do with the poem.
I agree that poems ought to stand alone—
my favorites do—but a little context
never ruined one, especially if the poem
really nails a thing, which is when
I look for the contributor's note anyway, as I did
after reading Bruce Weigl's "May,"
about putting his dog to sleep.
I got to the last line and turned
to the back hoping for one more glimpse
of the man who held the weight of that
dog in his arms, his head against hers
while the needle pricked the skin of her shaved leg.
What I got instead was a list, sterile
as the chrome table where May
took her last breath
and died.

What's Best

Some would say
if I want what's best
for our earth and oceans and future,
I should consume
no animal products,
or at least limit myself
to that which is produced humanely
and on a small scale.
I shouldn't eat grapes
picked by underpaid workers, grain
grown in razed forests.
I shouldn't consume anything
that has been transported a great distance,
shouldn't shop in stores
run by underpaid employees.
I shouldn't buy products
made of plastic, or wrapped,
and I shouldn't throw the plastic in the trash.
I shouldn't throw away aluminum,
tin, glass, paper, anything.
I shouldn't drive a car or fly on planes. I shouldn't
bear children, but if I must, I should
have only one, and I should not spoil it.
I shouldn't diaper the baby in disposables
or use water to wash cloth.
I shouldn't live in a big house and shouldn't
heat or cool it using electricity or gas.
I shouldn't dry my clothes in a dryer, take baths

or long showers. I shouldn't leave the tap running
while I wash dishes or brush my teeth.
I shouldn't water my yard on odd days, or even.
I shouldn't become attached to things and shouldn't
hoard them. I shouldn't enable addictions,
give unsolicited advice, get overstressed, consider drugs,
or commit suicide. I shouldn't judge others
or be too hard on myself. I shouldn't think
negative thoughts, complain, or fail
to appreciate how good I have it. I shouldn't
wonder if I should ever have been born.

The Day I Die

will be a Saturday or a Tuesday, maybe.
A day with a weather forecast,
a high and a low. There will be news:
a scandal, a disaster, some good
deed. The mail will come. People
will walk their dogs.

The day I die will be a certain
day, a square on a calendar page
to be flipped up and pinned
at the end of the month. It may be August
or November; school will be out or in;
somebody will have to catch a plane.

There will be messages, bills to pay,
things left undone. It will be a day
like today, or tomorrow—a date
I might note with a reminder, an appointment,
or nothing at all.

Everything Must Go

Pine bedroom furniture,
Dressers, nightstands, headboards,

Motorcycles, mobile homes, firewood
Seasoned and split, free delivery,

Purebred miniature schnauzer puppies,
Horses, loans, appliances large and small.

Eroded Pride, Wayward Dragon, Desire
To Die, industrial metal bands to play

Local bars. Singles' mixers, opportunities
To work at home, lose weight, quit

Smoking. Errand runners, babysitters,
Tax preparers, business cards fanned

Beneath tacks, phone-number fringed pages,
Laser-printed, pencil-scrawled, photo-illustrated,

Pinned and stapled one upon another,
Each its own float in a Christmas

Parade through the center of town
Or flying through the night sky,

Pulling not Santa upon his sleigh, but
The plain white sheet in the corner:

JOSHUA HONEST AND FAIR
GUTTER CLEANING
CHRISTMAS LIGHTS UP
ANY HELP NEEDED
I'M YOUR MAN
CREMATIONS FROM $899

Losing Teeth

I miss losing teeth,
the gradual loosening. Rocking
a tooth back and forth, day by day
the surrendering of the hold.
I miss the last hours
especially, the last hanging on
by ligaments, the sounds of tiny
rips, and the falling out—
or because I usually lacked patience—
the push, or the yank, the dental floss
noose, the slamming of the bathroom door,
the final tear.
And then the soft spot under:
pulp, not-quite-blister,
smooth, almost sweet to taste.
I miss the gap.
Something gone
where something was,
and the feel of the sides
of the neighbor teeth.
I miss cradling a tooth in my hand,
careful not to wash it down
the drain, rinsing off
the blood, the sharpness
of the root on my fingertip, putting
it dry in an envelope, offering it up,
coins under my pillow next morning.
I miss the nudge of the new

crown, one white ridge at a time.
The texture of new enamel.
I miss the second chance,
the in-between, the some
baby teeth, some permanent,
the halfway there, little by little,
my mouth renewing its cache, the thrill
of what I thought was growing up.

Leave Everything Behind

Leave everything behind, the loudspeaker says,
what we must do in the event
of an emergency landing.

I find myself glancing:
now at my stack of essays to grade,
now at the duffel beneath my seat,
now at the belongings others have carried on:
Laptop computers, money belts, the Chihuahua in a crate.

Stowed in the overhead compartments
and the seatback pockets:
Jewels, medications, passports.
Identification, necessities, and secrets—
things we cannot afford to give over, cannot risk
checking as baggage, risk their being searched
without us.

The nearest exit may be behind you, the speaker says,
Take a moment to locate it.

How quickly then, am I overcome
by uncertainty, how precarious our station,
passengers clutching these precious stones and documents,
as when sleep rescues me—rescues us all
from our waking selves for those hours
with their hurtling vastness, a plane
to carry us over an ocean, one day into another.

Everything Was Oddly the Same

September 12, 2001, Nevada

Bells rang at 8:30, noon, and three o'clock.
I taught my fourth graders, ate an orange at recess.
After school, I drove toward the swim center.
It was my routine: Wednesday, laps.
What else should I have done?

But on the highway, same as that morning
going to school, I felt some difference,
a camaraderie with other drivers.
We'd been hijacked, all of us, never
having imagined such a thing.
No one knew what would happen next.

Checking in at the pool, the woman in front of me
was out of cash. She dug through her purse—nothing
I would notice on a typical day. On a typical day,
I would stand there and wait.

But it was September the twelfth.
All planes were grounded, firefighters stood
on the sidewalk collecting money, people lined up
around city blocks to open their veins.
I had only watched news and news, gotten up
in the morning, packed a lunch, and gone to school,
where I said nothing to my students, who said nothing to me.
Across the continent, wreckage was smoldering.
I thought maybe I should live differently.

That moment—at the register, at the pool—
felt like a small chance. The woman out of cash
had barely begun to search her purse
when I said, "I'll pay."
And to the clerk, "Take it off my punch card."
No, no, said the woman.
"Yes, I'll get it." I held out my card.

The three of us looked at each other, the woman, the clerk, and I.
Our lives, at least, had been spared.
"Never mind." The clerk dropped his gaze
and waved us in. "You both go free."

Hotel Casino

Welcome Winners
   —On the door to John Ascuaga's Nugget,
   Sparks, Nevada

4. Casino: a chamber of sensory disorientation.

1. No visible clocks, doors, or windows. The bathroom always at the other end of a slot-machine maze.

9. Kaleidoscope carpet bounces off the ceiling and spins around rooted chairs.

3. Not every elevator goes to every floor.

11. A voice on the loudspeaker counts down: three minutes to go, one minute to go.

15.

81. Loose slots suck up your loose change.

6. You hear "Funkytown" and "Ruby Tuesday" playing at the same time.

16.

19.

7. "Keno?"

98. *Mi casino es su casino.*

20. The room's mouth never shuts.

31. You can leave a casino, but not without its scent in your hair.

Morning

The stillness, the radio's news,
the scent of rain. My neighbor
bending to pick up his newspaper
in its orange plastic bag, tossed
on the step. The cars all
heading this way or that,
a fine spray beneath their wheels. Vapor
rising from sidewalks, and the light
of the eastern sun, slanting long, as if
there's all the time in the world.

II.

Twelve Days of Christmas

One partridge in a pear tree sounds romantic,
I guess, but by the time she gets the turtle doves,
French hens, and calling birds, let's face it,
enough is enough. And how are all these sent,
by the way? Through the mail, by train?

The five golden rings I can see. One
for each finger and the thumb, if she's into
jewelry. But then we're right back
to fowl. Six geese—a-laying, no less—so
more on the way. Did her true love have his sights
set on a farm, or a zoo? Was this a warning
of what life with him would be?

And if he loves her so much, where is he anyway?
Couldn't he spend some of this money and effort
on coming to visit? But no, he sends an entourage
in his place. Eight maids a-milking, which I assume
includes the cows. Although, being maids,
they might at least help tend the birds.

Nine drummers drumming, ten pipers piping. All
those musical instruments, all the noise! And
is she having to put these people up? Personally,
I would have drawn the line a long time ago,
stopped answering the door, started marking parcels
Return to Sender. But maybe she wants to be gracious,
so I suppose if you can't beat them, join the eleven ladies

dancing. The twelve could pair up
with the lords a-leaping, all two dozen of them,
twirl away into the sunset, and leave
behind the honking chorus of birds.

Leone to Ben

I hope you know I've stayed by your side,
eaten the fruit cups and spaghetti, meals
they bring three times a day. Again and again
I say, *Thank you for sixty-six years,*
 you gave me a good life,
 you've been a good husband.

Our children came, sat with me, held your hand.
Bruce's eyes teared up the whole time—
I haven't seen him cry for fifty years.
Robin stayed all night. Our granddaughters
stood by your bed. Krista rested her head on your chest,
said into your good ear, *Don't try to answer.*
You've said all you need to say.
Robbi held the baby by your side,
guided her little hand to grasp your finger.
At the door told her, *Wave bye-bye.*

Last weekend the doctors told me, *A day or two,*
and here it is Thursday. You always did everything
in extremes. The boys drank too much milk,
so you brought home a cow. You wanted a garden,
so you traded our house for a farm. You worked
until two in the morning to get a job done, and now
your heart keeps beating without you.

I want to go home, sleep in our bed, sort the mail,
throw away the food rotting in the refrigerator.

But I don't even walk down the hall.
Any breath now could be your last.

As long as you're here, I have something
to do. When I go home, I will be a widow.

The Reception

They stand before a table
laid with the good silver,
homemade cake on a pedestal,
a sheer ribbon tied to the knife.
My mother wears a plain beige
dress, her curled hair sprayed firm.
My father is smiling,
eyes ahead and bright blue
as the blue of his jacket, a white rose
pinned to the lapel. Mother's darkened
lashes hide her eyes, looking down,
and she smiles, too—widely,
genuinely—neither of them posing.
It doesn't match what became her regrets:
no formal gown, so few guests,
the courthouse and the justice
of the peace. They look happy
and young, their teeth so white,
their faces smooth as children's.
They must have liked this picture,
one of few kept behind glass in a frame—mine,
now. I hold the shards of what was to come,
and this snapshot of their laughter—
perhaps about his having to climb
in a window for his shoes that day—
or perhaps they are nervous: new
bands of gold encircle their ring fingers,
his hand covers hers, and together

they slice through angel food,
whipped cream, strawberries
already halved.
The first task of marriage:
Take a knife. Cut up the sweet.

Would It Be So Wrong

to suggest that he move
next door? I don't want him
gone altogether, neither can I stand
him underfoot. It might be ideal
to holler over the fence,
invite him to dinner.
We'd sit together on the patio, eat
asparagus from his garden,
grilled shrimp under the setting sun,
then kiss the grease from our lips,
maybe more. After,
he'd go home
and watch basketball at full volume,
while I soak in the tub listening to Coltrane.
Then, wearing pajamas, hair uncombed,
I'd curl up in my own living
room with Robert Frost or People
and the cat, the quiet,
the light of a single lamp.

What's Your Favorite Animal?

This question from my mother-in-law,
this, what it has come to
after four days and four nights
of looking at linoleum samples,
praising her apple turnovers, hearing
details of Mrs. Crawford's bunions.

This question, from where
she sits in the back seat of the car
beside her husband, behind mine,
their son, who is at the wheel,
the band of silence between the men
wound like twine binding spools.
This question, her trying to break it:
What's your favorite animal, Krista?

On our way to dinner, hardly any traffic.
Rain spatters the windshield,
the wipers squeak, everyone is hungry.
In the darkness outside, our reflections
are grave, waiting for the answer
to a question I haven't considered
since seventh-grade Spanish.
My reply then must have been simple—
gato, vaca—some animal
whose name I knew.

Sea horses, I say, finally.
I like how the males carry the young.

The Counselor

We sit side by side on a love seat
across from her. I hug a needlepoint pillow
and fan my keys on the armrest:
office, mailbox, car, house, unknown.
She asks another question,
hands folded in her lap, the church
without the steeple. She wears a pearl
ring in rose gold, wedding band—
a complement to the brain coral, pale
pink and mounted on a stand
between reference books. My husband
doesn't have the answer, fails
once again to explain. His voice recedes
as my gaze drifts again toward the coral,
sea flower, cousin to anemones, the jelly,
skeleton of a living being—an animal
with the fortune of resembling
the mind: folds and channels
kneaded by attachment, stimulation,
pulse of water. Skeleton
of the beautiful, of something once
alive, that might have survived
two hundred years—how many
life spans, how many days—
living being, builder of reef,
home to smaller creatures, lifted
from the ocean, dried, affixed, displayed, sold.

Sacrament of Reconciliation

On the eve of my therapist's retirement,

   I dream she is a Catholic.

Her husband and I

         argue with her:

the virgin birth,

transubstantiation,

papal infallibility...

It's no use.
    She holds firm.

      Either she's just converted

or has managed to hide

        her faith all these years.

In any case, I know

    it's over between us.

How is she going to help me

if she believes

God is in control of everything?

Sands of Mint

after E. E. Cummings

my horse ran through sands of mint
through glaciers of luster through soons of whim
singeing each blade out of each flight
my horse galloped through breadths of dune

the arid shards of where and when
called skies aflame to throw their deep
plunged at his footfall to the gloaming's hill
lulled the grieving to amalgam's heat

my horse's mane combed his wake
for he could leap the water's pearl
lean as winter's lean and grace
no thirsty earth but gave his world

scattering the ankle of the mountain
my horse ran through dooms of stone
begging a chasm called the night
sparking will from cove to bloom

his muscle was muscle his lash was lash
no dying creature but turned the sky
no horse would give what's sent to gone
keening the spring of how and why

I Don't Know Any Stories

I don't know any stories, he replied
every time I said, curled under the covers
against his back, "Tell me a story."

A running joke. One of many
we stopped making,
toward the end, when we slept
on opposite shores of our
bed, drifted to rooms
on opposite sides of the house.

I was no longer there
to ask, and besides,
I had meant
tell me you imagine
we can survive,
why we're here,
who you are. Tell me
the impossible will be true:
you will change, you want to

love me. Promise, if nothing else,
one thing: promise you will leave.
You won't make me
make the last move. You won't
wait it out, won't settle.

Turn around. Kiss me,
smother me, rip
my nightgown off. Throttle me, even,
but don't lie
there, declining without trying.
Don't just lie there.
Don't tell me
you don't know.

Letter V

The v slices
divorce
di- spins down
to the left, alone
comes to sound
like *die*,
what you are
sure you want.
And -*orce*, cut off,
a spewed-out
syllable, a spiny
thing that rakes
your gut. What's left
is -v-, a blade
to carve all new
v's of your
body: armpit, elbow,
the cunt, the corners
of your mouth. The wells
between your toes, your fingers,
where the webbing
has evolved out, where now,
in place of your diamond—
a pale soft band of skin.

Only Now

do you begin to hear
everyone ask, *how are you?*
At the post office, the cash register,
on the phone, everywhere,
everybody asks—an unintended cruelty
when you're drowning in the unseen
chemistry of your brain, the unknown
substance of grief. A question
that keeps your resilience submerged,
your words forming bubbles
that rise to the surface and pop
before anyone hears.
Only here, where you scramble
for footing, do the words
how are you? amplify,
each a barbed hook that catches
in your mouth when you reply:
"Fine. And you?"

After

She begins grocery shopping
again, buys herself flowers:
bouquets of carnations for eight
ninety-nine, poinsettias at Christmas,
in March a white orchid in a plastic pot.
Someone in line says keep it somewhere
bright and humid, mist it twice a day.

In June, she brings home zinnias
with mountain aster and lemon leaf,
clears his magazines and the remotes
from the coffee table, and arranges
the blooms in a clear vase,
its reflection spilling through the surface.
The bases form the waist of an hourglass,
an equal amount of water in each bowl,
flowers reaching skyward and earthward.

Still life against the backdrop
of carved armoire, the whole of it
is pristine until the water grows cloudy,
pollen dusts the glass, and the first
zinnia droops—right before her eyes—
top-heavy, unable to bear
the burden of uprightness, the stem
bends and the bloom faces its mirror.

Prolate Spheroid

Football is a complex
game of strategy
full of plays
I don't appreciate.
To me, one scene compares
closely with the next:
men in tights chase a ball
and each other. Two sit
across from an alien exec
who keeps repeating "Fed Ex"
since *that's all you need to know.*
They do group hugs, dog piles.
A schnauzer bites a man's crotch
at the command "Budweiser,"
which sends the victim's beer sailing
into the master's hands.
Short bursts of helmet crashing
follow a woman with near-bare breasts
who promises, "See you at half time."
A donkey interviews
with the Clydesdales to help pull
the Budweiser wagon for those
unconvinced by the crotch bite.
Officials deliberate, one of them
announces the call: booming words
accompany mysterious hand signals,
and Charmin trails from a coach's pants.
Women with pom-poms cheer,

others play bikini volleyball
on a snow-covered beach to prove
Visa really can buy anything.
After a Hail Mary pass, children
must eat soap for saying "Holy Shh . . ."
about the new Chevrolet convertible.
A fake punt fails,
but it's the old couple who fight
over the Frito-Lays
who get to me. I never liked chips
and suddenly I want some.

Fans of My Unconscious

I come upon a school in the desert, the same school where I taught years ago, so I know this is the place, although it is surrounded by lush green fields. It is early summer, the temperature cool and the daisies in bloom. To the west a small log cabin. I don't remember this cabin at all, but I go into it on an errand, to file a paper. I notice some things inside that I must have stored there and forgotten: my cloisonné vase, the fishbowl, a stack of monogrammed linens. In a pull-out couch that is actually a trunk, I find all sorts of treasures. Silver serving dishes, china cups and saucers, and a miniature scratching tree for the cats, like the one at home that has the peaked roof. I'm happy to see that, happy to see all of it, so neatly and lovingly packed, untouched for all the years I was away.

Outside, I try to sort everything and gather what is mine. People start coming around, dozens of people, curious; it seems the cabin has not been opened in years. Will they think this is a yard sale, all of this up for grabs? I have to be quick. I have not missed these things, yet now I cherish them, and I want to get them home. There's nothing to do but take charge before something goes missing. I stand on the front porch, like a president on a whistle-stop tour. "Everyone, please listen up. I need to tell you what happened here." They soon hush. "I worked at this school many years ago. I was worried about my marriage at that point, it had started to go downhill." I make a motion with my thumb, swooping down. "I hoped it would go back uphill, but I was afraid it wouldn't, so I asked the principal if I could store some things here." I indicate the cabin. "He was kind enough to let me use this space. So I took some time off and during that time, I got divorced, and I forgot what I had left. But now I'm back, and I came upon these things, and I remembered. Now if you guys would be so kind as to help me load them up—" Before I finish, they begin to rally and cheer. They are very happy for me, and they help.

Dietary Restrictions

She makes me want to wear a pork chop around my neck.
   —Joan, colleague and attempted convert of Augusta

After Cyn's funeral, I think I'll slaughter a pig in the kitchen.
   —Michael, foodie, nonobservant Jew, and devoted
   husband of Cynthia

I.

Augusta consumes no animal products in any form
whatsoever and implores everyone to do the same.

Amy eats no raw broccoli.

Greg, only organic.

Cathy eats no refined sugar and no flour
of any grain or tuber.

Other than shrimp, Amanda eats no legged being.

Frank eats no wheat, rye, or barley.

Milana eats no peanuts, no eggs, and no food
processed on equipment shared with these.

Terri eats no flesh and no hoof.

Cyrus abstains from processed foods
packaged in boxes and bags.

Cynthia keeps strictly kosher, maintaining
separate utensils for milk, meat, and Passover.

Anya catches herself if she uses a lobster net
even as a metaphor.

II.

You are what you eat,
and if I eat better than you,
well . . .

III.

For me, it used to be no high-fat foods,
no garlic, onions, cauliflower, cabbage, beans,
eggs, milk, carbonated drinks, or hard candies.

But since my first marriage, my gut
feels better and now I allow myself any food
as long as I eat it mindfully:
Not as reward or consolation;
not while driving, reading,
writing, watching a screen, or feeling
I want to escape something. I aspire
never to feel too hungry, never too full,
to sit down and enjoy what I eat
to the greatest extent the moment allows,
and, above all, to forgive myself
when I don't.

I eat what I want when I want it
on a sliding scale:
it has to be worth the cost.

IV.

What I *want*, not necessarily what I crave.

V.

After the divorce, I managed
to have dinner with a string of men
who were current or former vegetarians.
Over lamb curry, Lester explained
he had lasted five years, but a craving
for sausages eventually did him in.

Robert remembered where he was and who with
each time he'd tasted a particular cut.
At my kitchen table, he ate with me his first tri-tip
in years, and when he pointed this out, it seemed the time
to ask what made him decide to eat meat again.

"The world's going to end
in a big fiery ball anyway," he said.

As good an argument as any I've heard
for eating what you like.

The next spring, I met my new love,
Scott, who confessed he was dying
to order fried shrimp, but unfortunately,
he was a vegetarian.

"Well," I said, "you have something
to look forward to."

Patio Tomatoes

I.

My boyfriend leaves his patio tomatoes
at my apartment at around the three-year mark,
just when I'm realizing he may never commit.
This arrangement is supposed to be temporary,
while we're out of town, so my neighbor can water
since he doesn't know any of his neighbors
well enough to ask. Which maybe should be a sign.
We return from the trip, I am still ringless,
and he leaves the tomatoes with me. I decide
this is a metaphor: Anything involving commitment
is my problem. On cue, winter blows in and the plant dies.
I bring in the last of the fruits and set them in a bowl.
I think, *patio tomatoes. Tomatoes designed for a person*
lacking a patch of earth, a person whose level of settledness
is a patio. Biting into one, I notice the skin is thick and tough,
the taste unremarkable. *Patio tomato: while it needs*
care, it is not confined by its roots. I carry it easily to the trash.

II.

The plant has been gone three weeks and the fruits just as long
in their bowl. I'm keeping my distance. Once I stop calling,
my phone starts ringing. Sometimes I don't answer,
even turn off my machine. Let him wonder
where I am. I mean to write about the tomatoes, to record

their decay as it occurs, but I set them on top of the fridge
and forget them until I'm up there retrieving a vase
for roses. The tomatoes have collapsed and darkened.
I must have left three store-boughts in the mix—
there are stickers bearing the SKU 4664.
One store-bought is red and plump, passable, even.
It could be at the grocery, overlooked. It attaches
by the stem to another tomato that has shriveled
and grown a white collar of fuzz. The healthier
tomato appears to have sucked the life from this one.
A vampire tomato. The patio tomatoes?
They look like sundried, only black and crisp.
As if next, they will turn to ash.

III.

Come February, he goes and ruins the whole metaphor
by marrying me. Unfortunately for this poem,
we've been happy ever since. The morning of our third
anniversary, I rise at five to write. We've moved
from the apartment to our house, and yes, I wrapped
the bowl of tomatoes in newspaper when I packed.
They've been taking up the back quarter of a desk drawer
ever since. Only the stickers remain unchanged.
In fact, without that dried-up vampire stem, they'd be
unrecognizable. Yet I seem unable to let them go.
I begin with the mold, the solidified collar, the puffy trails
that look like miniature storm clouds. No, maybe
I should start with the dark rings that stain
the bowl, ghosts of fruits' original shape.

Frankly, a photograph would do better justice.
But who wants to look at a bowl of three-year-old tomatoes,
going on four? Who keeps such a thing? And how could I
explain this to anyone who has a practical use
for early mornings? Someone who is cooking stew
in a crock pot, folding laundry, or working out.
I was up early today wondering which to describe,
the fruits or the mold. I kept a bowl of tomatoes
so I could write about them as they rotted.

I Love You

*Are you ever afraid you'll accidentally say "I love you" to a telemarketer
or a customer service person when you're about to hang up?*
— Scott Lukas, inadvertently offering one more
reason why he prefers e-mail

A phrase thrown out casually
over landlines, between
cell phone towers,
sometimes garbled
on a faulty connection,
sometimes truncated,
mainly spoken when guaranteed
to be returned ... *you too.*
Guilty of overuse, I say it often
knowing any opportunity to say it
may be my last—I could die,
or they could—but I try not to
say it with that in mind.
I say it because I mean it,
and out of habit, and also,
by now, it's expected
and to leave it unsaid
would be more significant
than simply to say it once more.

Husbands

Terri's loses the caps to things.
She's forever fitting bits of foil
on bottles of olive oil and vinegar.

Sandra's does all the dishes,
and the rule is, if it's your job,
you get to do it your way
in your own time. She doesn't nag,
knowing how it feels since her ex nagged her.
Luckily, since she cooks, the other rule is,
if she says I need the kitchen clean, he does it.

Janie's ex didn't do anything
except make a lot of money and change
the oil in both cars. She was teaching half-time,
doing the rest full-time. When it was over,
she promptly paved the backyard of her new place.
He now has a gardener, a maid, a pool guy,
and the kids on alternate weekends.

My ex didn't earn a living for five
of the nine years, but he made a good lasagna
and could fix anything—except me.
Like Sandra's ex with her, he didn't love me
enough, though unlike hers, he never
phrased it as such. The fact was the ex
and I are too alike: overly serious, always thinking
everything has to be finished first.

My new is the one to insist on date nights.
He wants to cuddle (yes, that's his word)
before the dishes and go on trips
ahead of retirement. He has managed
to loosen me up. My only regret
is not meeting him first, but cliché would argue
if I had, I might not be thanking my lucky stars
every single day. I try to remember that

when he uses metal on Teflon. When he won't clean
the gasket of the washing machine or squeegee
the corners of the shower door, when he won't hang up towels
or scrub his night guard. The stains and the odors—well,
they're nothing, surely, compared to living with me.

Vade Mecum

You can run your hand along my binding, trace
the raised letters of my title, take off my dust jacket,

      feel the texture, the roughness of my fore-edge.
      Lay me down on my spine, lay me down

on your table, or cradle me
between your knees, take me

      to your bed. Breathe in the scent
      of my paper, feel how smooth my pages,

open me and dip in—notice my dedication,
advance praise—skim the body

      do what you can to resist
      skipping to the end. Read me all the way

through. Read me from the beginning, let go
your disbelief, let anticipation build. Trust me

      to surprise you. Get entangled,
      lose yourself in the rising action,

keep going, keep going through my climax,
through the fall, the denouement.

      And after, hold me. Stay with me, hold me,
      and drift to sleep dreaming my words, cover to cover.

III.

On the Staircase, 1961

The woman who will become
my mother sits behind bars
of a wrought-iron railing.
Barely a teenager,
the skin still smooth around her eyes,
black hair obscured in the smoke
of shadows at her back,
fingers—still bare of rings—
splayed on her thigh,
the scrollwork's shadow cast
across her chest, an albatross.
I would have thought she'd look hopeful
that one day she'll marry the right man,
have the children, the home she dreams of.
But her gaze is hard, as if she knows
what she will do, how she will lose
her brothers, husbands, daughters,
lose friends like kindling dropped
to feed the smolder of her undoing.
As if the camera's flash
were a warning,
at this instant, I see
she knew
and she chose.

True Is What You Remember

It was Christmas morning. Crumbs speckled the plate we left for Santa. Mom sat beside the tree in her bathrobe as Dad built a fire in the Franklin stove. There were puppets, a Slinky, dolls we could feed and change. The sun rose sparkling on snow drifts beneath the windows. On TV was a choir singing, "Jingle Bells," "Joy to the World," the volume turned down low. Crumpled paper lay scattered on the carpet; cups of coffee steamed in Mom and Dad's hands. On the tree there were lights like tiny firecrackers. We had breakfast—sweet rolls, cranberry juice—a green checkered cloth on the table. Mom brought sliced oranges, sugar, a pitcher of milk. We fought over who would play with the Slinky first. The weather came on between carols. Mom cleared everything away. She put her hand on Dad's shoulder and he turned from her, stood up quickly. The volume of the television rose with a commercial. He changed the channel and began to watch the news. I nudged you under the table and we slid from our chairs. Mom came in the living room with a sack for garbage. She began to fill it with boxes, torn paper, and ribbon. We played school with the puppets. I was the teacher since I'd been in kindergarten; you were going on four next month. We said it would be more fun with Amy and Angela. We couldn't wait to show them our new toys. Mom must have heard. She sank to the couch, let the bag of waste paper slip to the floor and spill. She began to cry. "It's Christmas morning and all you can talk about is your friends. You don't even want to be with me." We stopped. Our hands dropped to our sides, the puppets' hair hung straight to the floor. We watched her a moment, and then I leaned to pick up another, flaccid in its box, offered it to her. "Let's play house then. You be the mom."

I Forget Her Name

In gymnastics with me, there was a girl
whose mother had died. Somehow
I knew this, had heard it from someone.

The girl had blond hair, long and shiny
as corn silk, and she didn't act like her mother had died.
But I noticed her dad always picked her up after class,
not like everyone else, whose moms came.
There was no other proof that this horrible thing was true.

So one day, after balance beam, we're in line
waiting our turn on the parallel bars, and she's behind me.
I've never stood this close to her, never had a chance
to talk to her, and all I can think about is her dead mother.

After a moment, I turn and say,

      Backward bends are hard. Do you ever practice at home?

"Sometimes," she says.

      Do you show your parents?

She nods and begins to redden and shift from foot to foot.

This girl doesn't know me, wouldn't know
I know, but I can't stop now. I want to know it
from her. I want some sure sign, so I ask,

What does your mom say about it?

Instantly, there are tears, and I forget
what happened next.
I don't think she ran.
I didn't reach out
to touch her shoulder.

I hope, now, that
I stopped. Just turned around
and left her alone.

But this I know:
There was something
like a thrill in seeing it was true,
seeing it was right there
with her. All the time,
during warm-up
and balance beam
and when she laughed, and standing in line,
it was there.

War, Hunger, and Accidents Aside

I would go back and play when my sister asked,
or erase what I wrote to Kim.

I'd replace word searches with real
history, read more classics, perhaps

enroll in private school. Open my father's
arms—keep my parents married,

put one of them in charge.
Give my mother a friend,

undo some damage, decline
Sixto's invitation. I'd take

my virginity back from Diederick,
start treatment sooner, major

in English, turn around halfway
up Mount Tallac, rent my own

place. Postpone marriage, reconsider
orthodontics, take my time. Forget all this.

I would begin at the beginning, a baby,
curled in my mother's arms.

This time, she'd set the bottle
aside and feed me from her breast, milk

to prime the unfolding of what we
lack, to fill the gulf between us.

A Girl at Ten

after Donald Justice

A girl at ten
Begins to throw open doors

To rooms she may wish to inhabit.
Standing on the threshold, she feels

A pull beneath her feet like sand
At the shore, waves lapping around her ankles.

And with a glance in the mirror
She catches sight of a woman's lips mouthing

Her mother's words out in the open
And that mother's skin,

Still smooth with the invincibility of youth.
More girl than woman,

Something calls her, something from a great distance
Like daybreak's glimmer

Of sun, reckless
Blazing the edge of an unclaimed coast.

September

Evening gray sifts through flesh-pink
clouds, fading light scattered
on the patio before the porch swing,
where I sit beside my mother
and grandmother, where we have lingered
at twilight other days. Now
looking at their profiles, I see
the time-progressed sketch of my own:

same nose and blue eyes, the shape
of our face giving way to wrinkles,
chestnut hair thinning to white.
We are one woman

between facing mirrors. We cannot see
around our body, past
where the tunnel
takes a turn, unknown
passageway for the train we await here

on the patio. We talk of memories,
the breeze, the birch leaves
turning colors of a sunset.

Some must have boarded, or will,
ahead of their mothers, and some together,
but as far back as we can see
each of us has gone in order, each
taking the place of the last.

Now or Then

Grandma, just shy of ninety-one,
thinks she is twelve again, or maybe twenty,
asks for the hundredth time,
Have you seen my folks?
I'm worried sick—I haven't
heard from them all day.

Long dead when I was born, they live
in black-and-white photographs, her stories.

Back when she remembered,
she would tell about camping, how
they'd drive the Packard
on gravel roads from San Francisco
to Monterey, Big Sur, one time up to Canada.
How her mother sewed their sleeping bags
with sand dollar–sized buttons along the edge.
How her daddy tied his shaving mirror
to a tree. They slept in a canvas tent, stored meat
in a basket lined with asbestos
and tin, used milk bottles to hold water.

They're fine, I tell her. *They're all right.*
Her hand feels soft in mine, her skin
papery and thin.

My grandma knows a world
without zippers, nylon, the atomic bomb.
If you ask her what today is,
she says, *Well . . . yesterday,*
it was tomorrow.

Lion on Gold Coast

Squaw Valley, USA

Six years old, I say, I *want*
to ride alone, and Dad lets me.
Whisked from him, I hug the side pole.
The chair swings, waves
of snowflakes whip over the crest of the hill,
swirl in on themselves, wind tunnels
that could suck me away.
I look over my shoulder, see Dad,
his collar zipped against the cold.
I wish I could jump to his chair, feel his arm
around me. Gusts slash the air, roaring;
my nose pours, icy needles sting my face
barely exposed between neck-warmer and goggles.
Through steamed-up lenses, I squint at the red
sign posted to a distant tower, until
finally, I make out the words I've been
waiting for: Ski Tip Up.
I push myself from the chair,
face the slope,
and ski into the mouth of a lion.

I Dream of Osama bin Laden

My Carson City apartment is in Southern California.
I am my current age, although actually a kid again, living
with Dad, who isn't my real-life dad, but at the same time,
he is, and in any case, I'm dependent on him. We are hiding
Osama bin Laden from the government or for the government—
whatever the case, we can't let on he is here.

I must be a small child, because even though I'm thirty-seven,
at some point I am sitting in Dad's lap, saying I'm afraid
of having Osama bin Laden here, he's a murderer, etc.
Dad, as with most things, is not too worried about it.
Somehow, the way Osama is locked in is by ice.
A dubious system, in my opinion.

So I come home one day, and I go to open Osama's door,
which is the bathroom door and the bathroom door is locked.
"He's going to stay in there for two weeks,"
Dad says, no mention of getting him food or anything.

There is a tennis court and a chain-link fence
in the apartment. I'm wearing a white tennis dress, and Osama
asks me to climb the fence, presumably so he can look up
my dress. Given his religion, I know he normally wouldn't
lay eyes on a woman (other than his wives, mother, sisters)
who is not completely covered, let alone peek up her dress.
But I must not be that surprised because next
I say, Sure, I could climb the fence, but not in my bare feet—
what I have at the moment.

It's one thing to have Osama on the other side
of a chain-link fence, but I get nervous that night
to find him and his wife camped out in my bedroom. Politeness
is a strain, but I try making small talk as I turn on my computer.
My e-mail contains five messages from an anonymous sender,
one a detailed map with the route highlighted from the
apartment to his target somewhere in San Diego. Two others read only,
"I know what you're thinking."

Smile Lines

The wrinkles
that have been
invisible are visible,
now I'm
nearly forty.
The sunburns
of my youth
surface in the
fissures of age.
It's like that,
isn't it? With stars,
too. The gleam
now reaching
my eyes
first on its way
light years ago.

IV.

A Childless Woman

Thus defined by her lack.

While *mother* tells all, serving
as both noun and verb, *childless* alone
is a modifier, needing further explanation.

Nulligravida, a woman who has never been
pregnant, and nullipara, one who hasn't given
birth, come from New Latin *nullus*, no, not any.
Unwieldy textbook terms, and insufficient
when you consider adoptive mothers.

So I say we need a word
and I propose *witch*.
It is as witches that we first appear
to children, is it not? Living alone
in the forest, ready to lure them in
and eat them? Demanding their hearts
delivered in a box made of jewels?

In the same tales, the mothers
are dead, replaced by the evil
wives of hapless fathers, desperate
for someone to look after the children.
The stepmothers work them like slaves, threaten
to abandon them in the woods.

Wouldn't you rather be the witch,
your walls made of gingerbread? The simplicity
of cooking in one pot? Perhaps vulnerable
to being crushed by a falling house, but free—
your broom meant for flying.

Baby Shower

Bathroom humor is lost on me,
watching a blindfolded pregnant woman
remove a peanut-butter-smeared diaper
from a doll and wipe its plastic rear.
We all laugh while I lament
this harbinger of conversations to come.
Watching soon-to-be Mother
open presents, I concur that tiny jeans,
socks, and hooded towels are so *cute!*
I just don't want to snatch
fuzzy ducky clothespins off the blouses
of guests who say the word.
She who gets the most wins a prize,
as does she who can recall and list
all the items in the Safety 1st Froggy Tub.
Moms can name the specialized pumps, slings, and pads,
while the best I can do is "rattle" and "pacifier."
In exchange for my gift, *The Children's Treasury*
of Verses, I get a friend who will soon become
two people, both as yet unknown.
And I am given a night sky cut-out to write my wish
upon a star for Baby: May he love
to read. Placed in a scrapbook among hopes
for a long life, friends, and good fortune.
My wish for Mother is not asked for
and must remain unsaid—that she not disappear
from me, that she not be swallowed up by the child.

Swimming Inside the Lines

My lane of choppy water
is cordoned off by a buoy line
that doesn't block the view
of teenage couples, trunks
pressed to string bikinis.

The guard's shrill whistle
keeps people out of my path but fails
to stop beach balls from bouncing
off my head, or to filter

debris. Aquatic dust bunnies bob in corners,
clumps of knotted hair float
over the tiled line I follow.
My earplugs muffle the shrieks and
laughter of kids, faces sticky with popsicle juice.
They ride pool noodles, do cannonball
dives, come up breathless
from tea parties and somersaults.

Pop tunes blast above the din
but nothing drowns out my heartbeat,
gasp of my breath every third stroke,
rhythm that calls to mind

this same pool Sunday mornings at eight,
sleepy lifeguards, scent of chlorine, clean
water, stillness broken
by the methodic kicks of grown-ups
swimming back and forth, back and forth.

Mother Goose

Where is Thumbkin? Where is Thumbkin?

My niece's favorite nursery rhyme.

She sits on my lap and we sing

Here I am, here I am

between brushings and braidings

of her fine blond hair.

How are you today, sir?

"Auntie, do you have any kids?"

"I have you."

Very well, I thank you.

"Silly, I mean your own kid."

"Oh . . . do you think I need one?"

Run away, Run away.

"Silly, every mother needs a baby."

Gifted and Talented

For my teaching license, I am required
to take a class called "Mainstreaming,"
in which we learn about every kind
of kid who could walk or be wheeled
through our future classroom doors.

Not the blind, the deaf, and the handicapped,
but students with
blindness, deafness, developmental delays,
autism, moderate to severe
learning disabilities, hyperactivity,
attention deficit, oppositional defiance
disorder, and so on.

The instructor, an elementary
principal by day, who outlines
each chapter and reads to us
these outlines each Wednesday
from six to nine, devotes
one hour one night to the subject
of students with
gifts and talents, who might also
come through our future.

Regarding special programs
for such students, one teacher-candidate asks,
"Do you have to be gifted to teach them?"

"No." The principal-instructor
shakes her head, as if
such a thing would be impossible.
"Not many gifted people
go into education."

The First Year

I. Rite of Passage

The boys' school where I taught
my first year. Twelve
to a class, by housing unit.
They wore pressed pants,
shirts, and matching ties,
their hair cut above the ears.

They were rapists, car thieves,
drug dealers, ages 14–18.
Most had a mother,
a grandmother, an aunt,

a woman, somewhere.
Many had babies; few, fathers.
They had the given names
of poets and professionals and saints:

Virgil, Michael, and José.
"Graves," "McCormick," "Lebron."
Full names they wrote in gang
calligraphy I was not supposed to allow.

II. "Are you a virgin?"

This was the worst it got, that first day,
when I gave each boy a strip

of paper and said to write me a question,
fold it up, and put it in the hat.
No names.

How old are you?
Do you go to parties?
What car do you drive?
You ever been locked up?

I promised to answer six
questions. When I unfolded
Are you a virgin? I read,
"What's your favorite ice cream?"
and answered, "Cherry."

III. Easley

I never knew who was in for what,
but I learned where they were from:
East LA, Fresno, San Jose.

Easley was from Oakland. A tall
black kid, one who needed
one-on-one for remedial reading.

We sat side by side bent over Laubach
books, and we talked between paragraphs
when I could see he needed a break
from sounding out words.
"The only thing wrong back home," he said,
"is too many guns."

He'd been shot at,
but I was the one who jumped
from my chair when a spider crawled across his book
that day. I wouldn't sit
back down until it was dead.

Among Professionals

We all know schadenfreude,
but is there a word for the satisfaction
we take in pointing out we are the ones
who have it the worst?

If I put in sixty hours a week, you do eighty.
If you have endless spreadsheets,
my jaw aches from smiling at clients.
If you have a larger caseload than last year,
I have no window in my office.
If I have no window, you've had a sniper
drill, and I ought to appreciate
my solid walls. If I have recess duty
on a freezing cold morning, you stay
until midnight catching up. If your boss
fails to understand your reports,
well, mine won't even reply to my questions.

How we love to tell of our travails,
to slip them in at the opportune moment.
Love their handiness when we wish
to decline an invitation or hang up the phone.
We even close our e-mails *Crazy busy,*
Better get back to work, or *Ten papers down,*
eight thousand forty-three to go . . .

Is it that we suffer from career-identity over-reliance?
Do we fear perceived availability?

Or should we blame our Puritan roots? Might it be simple
one-upmanship masquerading as commiseration?

I am tired of the endless labors, the bad boss.
I wonder, who among us will dare to withhold
mention of his toil. Who would boast
of work's pleasures instead?
Tell the secret thing you love about it,
the thing that makes you feel you're getting away
with something. Or at least admit to the benefits—
paid days off, or flexibility; the salary, or freedom
to answer only to yourself. What about the sanctioned
break from your kids, having the keys to a building
besides your house? Think of it. You belong
somewhere outside your own self. You have an easy
answer when asked, *What do you do?*

No Longer Miss B

I stand with my friend Susan, scanning
for theater seats, when I hear, "Miss B?"

I turn to see a young woman,
one of my students when I taught third grade.
Her red hair has become straight and brown,
her face slopes at odd angles
against my recollection, like a song
played live, dissonant
with the version my ear expects.

"Rachel?" I have to look
up to meet her eyes.
"You're so tall."
I ask what grade she's in, *eighth*,
and her favorite subject, *drama*.

Five years ago,
she would have squealed, clapped,
thrown her arms around me.
Once, when I said I'd be away at a conference
the next week, Rachel slumped
in her chair, demanding to know, *Why, why?*
"So I can become a better teacher."
But that's not possible! She pounded her desk.

Now she holds a playbill, nods vigorously
when I ask if she still likes to write, but her eyes

give her away. She wants to get back
to her friends. And without the classroom's
backdrop and pedestal, I am no longer
Miss B.
I wear blue jeans.
My friend is waiting. Our
smiles stiffen. There is nothing
more to say.

Composing a Sample Poem for Third Graders, Who Are Generally Encouraged to Write Cheerful Things, I Choose My Estranged Brother and the Color Gray

after Barbara M. Joosse, author of I Love You the Purplest

Ben, I love you the grayest.
I love you the color of forgotten things, cobwebs, and dust in corners.
I love you the color of storm clouds and thunder,
stripes on the june bug's wing.
I love you the color of driftwood, of ancient boulders
ground to bits by time and water.
Smoke, skyscrapers, and overwashed whites.
The color of a moth, pale cousin to the butterfly.
I love you the color of in-between, the color of a question
with no right answer.
I love you, Ben, the grayest.

Meadow's Rules

for my niece, Meadow, age three

When we play, the rules empty into one
another like our trips across your bedroom
to Hawaii. You've packed a suitcase.
When I get hungry on the plane, you offer
a plastic block of strawberry ice cream;
I lick the air—*delicious.*

No sooner am I snoring in our hotel
than you announce it's time
to take the bus home. *All the way
across the ocean?* "Yes," you say,
"But you can rest while I clean up."

Before my eyes close, you toss
the plastic Hoover aside
and arrange my seat, a floor pillow
by the dresser. Buckling up, I ask
the driver to slow down, but
he can't hear. He has too many teeth.

On another flight, we find a pen,
and you say we have to start
the list. For everyone in the family,
you make squiggles on a page and then ask
what else we should write down. I suggest the dog,
a tennis racket, a dishwasher. You accept
with a new squiggle or explain the obvious: "No.

There has to be two dishwashers
in the house." *Good point, I say.*
And we wouldn't want turtles on the list.

"Yes, we do. Put him by your name."
You thrust the paper into my hands and point,
and there I am, a thin blue noodle
swimming down the page.

My Niece

Born on the first day of spring the first
year of the millennium. Imitator of waitresses
and magicians; unpredictable thrower
of tantrums; connoisseur of Gummy Bears,
vanilla yogurt, and orange juice with calcium;
disliker of onions; wearer of snowsuits,
heart-shaped sunglasses, and undone braids;
speaker of nonsensical phrases; expert snorter;
constant storyteller; voracious imaginer
of the impossible: backyard roller coasters, airplanes
in the living room. *Oh, these are my taxes*,
she says when asked about papers
brought home from preschool one day.
Moderate taker of naps in the backseats of cars;
mess-maker of any room in her path;
blue-eyed, fair-haired angel quick-to-turn-
miserable scowler; tough-footed sprinter on beaches
and lawns; climber of slides; blower of bubbles
in bathtubs and swimming pools; granddaughter,
great-granddaughter, cousin, and big sister; turner
into her mother's shoulder, turner into her mother's leg;
frequent requester of big tickles and little
tickles; answerer of telephones real and pretend;
self-appointed CEO of seating arrangements
at all tables; drawer of a line in the sand
around beach toys and her brother and me.
Hey, guys, she says, *this is our property line, okay?*

What Box?

The Superintendent
wants to improve
our program, research
how it's done
in other districts.
We don't have to
reinvent the wheel,
she says. *It's time*
to think outside the box.
What box? I want to ask.
Are we in a box,
and are we thinking
inside it? Because
I see no box
and no thinking, actually.
Does one ever think
inside a box?
Would it not be cramped?
In fact, how about
thinking inside a box?
That would be different.
I think I'll propose that.
I propose that we think
inside boxes—about wheels
and not reinventing them.
Or, if the Superintendent
prefers, we could stand
outside our boxes,

with our wheels, and think
about them—but not
reinvent them, because
they're already invented.
In fact, forget standing,
we could sit back
and enjoy our wheels
outside our boxes.
We could even
put the wheels
on our boxes,
since we are outside them,
and they aren't
weighed down
by us. Yes!
We could
put the wheels
we didn't reinvent
on the boxes
we're thinking outside of,
and they could roll
away, of their own accord,
because we're thinking
outside the box,
not inside it.
And we don't
have any ideas.

About the Author

Krista Lukas' poem, "Letter from My Ancestors" was selected by Guest Editor Billy Collins for inclusion in *The Best American Poetry 2006*. She is the recipient a 2007 Nevada Arts Council Fellowship and the 2008 Robert Gorrell Award for Literary Achievement. Her book manuscript was a finalist for the May Swenson Poetry Award and the Pearl Poetry Prize.

Krista was born in Truckee, California, and grew up at Lake Tahoe. She received her Bachelor of Arts in Literature from University of California, San Diego in 1992. She teaches elementary school in Northern Nevada, where she lives with her husband, Anthropologist Scott A. Lukas.

COLOPHON

Designed and produced by Robert Blesse at the Black Rock Press, Department of Art, School of the Arts, University of Nevada, Reno.

The typeface used for the text is Joanna, a transitional serif typeface designed by Eric Gill in 1931 and named for one of his daughters. It was described by Gill himself as, "a book face free from all fancy business."

Printed and bound at BookMobile, Minneapolis